# Contents





**Glossary words**

When a word is printed in **bold**, you can look up its meaning in the Glossary on page 31.

# The sport

Surfing is an action-packed sport performed by skilled professionals. It is also a fun leisure activity enjoyed by many beach-goers. When we hear the word surfing, we usually think of surfboard riding, but there are other forms of surfing. Surfboard riding is a popular form of surfing, but bodyboarding, also known as boogie boarding, has developed into a very popular sport too, especially with younger children and teenagers.

Surfing is a popular competitive sport, and the best surfers in the world compete for prize money on the World Championship Tour.

**Did you know?**

***The first surfing World Championship was held in 1964 and was won by Australian surfer Bernard 'Midget' Farrelly.***

**People surf at beaches around the world, such as this one on Hatteras Island, North Carolina, United States of America.**

## The history of surfing

Surfing has been popular for hundreds of years. In the 1780s, the English explorer Captain James Cook saw Hawaiian people riding waves on large wooden planks. It was not until 1915, however, that Hawaiian Duke Kahanamoku introduced the surfboard to the rest of the United States of America and Australia. Since then, the popularity of surfing has grown dramatically, and people are now surfing in just about every country that has a coastline and breaking waves.

**Duke Kahanamoku (right) is often called the founder of modern surfing.**

## Riding the waves

In any type of surfing, the aim is to catch as many waves as possible and to ride these waves for as long as possible. When a surfer catches a wave, the aim is to begin riding near the **peak** of the wave. Once up and riding, the surfer uses the speed and power of the wave to perform manoeuvres and tricks on the wave **face**. Beginners can enjoy surfing on waves that are about 1 metre high. Riding really big waves calls for great skill and courage and is for more experienced surfers.

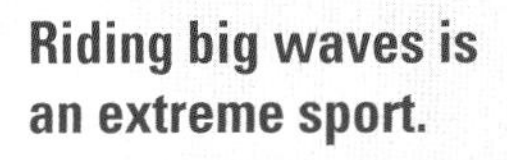

**Riding big waves is an extreme sport.**

# Equipment

The equipment that a surfer needs depends on the type of surfing. Surfboard riders use a surfboard and bodyboarders use a bodyboard.

## The surfboard

A surfboard is made of **fibreglass** and measures from 1.5 metres to 3 metres long. Surfboards come in two basic designs. The first, most popular type is a short-board or thruster. It has a pointy nose and three fins. The second, easier board to ride is a long-board or Malibu. It has a rounded nose and one fin. The part of the board that a surfer stands on is the **deck**. The sides are known as **rails**.

All surfboards have the same features, but the length and shape vary.

## The bodyboard

A bodyboard is made from a rubbery, foam-like material. Bodyboards measure from 97 to 117 centimetres long. The deck, or top surface, is hard-wearing and provides grip, while the bottom is very slick and provides speed. The nose of a bodyboard is flat, whereas the tail is curved.

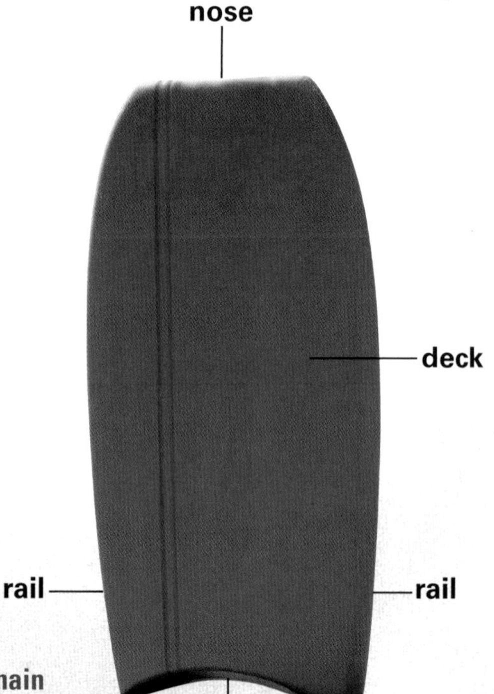


These are the main features of a bodyboard.

## Leg-ropes and leashes

Surfboard riders wear leg-ropes, which are long rubber cords that are about 1.8 metres long and have a padded strap at one end. The strap is fastened around the ankle of the surfer's back leg. The other end of the leg-rope is attached to the rear of the surfboard.

A leash is similar to a leg-rope and is used by bodyboard riders. A leash is about half as long as a leg-rope and is connected to the bodyboarder's wrist or forearm. Both leg-ropes and leashes are used to connect the surfer to the board so that they do not become separated after a **wipe-out**. They also protect other surfers and swimmers from being hit by flying boards.

A leash connects the bodyboarder's arm to the board.

## Wax and tailpads

The deck of a new surfboard is very smooth. When water gets on it the surface can become quite slippery. Surfers rub wax on the decks of their boards to give them more grip when riding a wave. Some surfers also stick rubber tailpads to the tails of their boards to give them better back-foot grip.

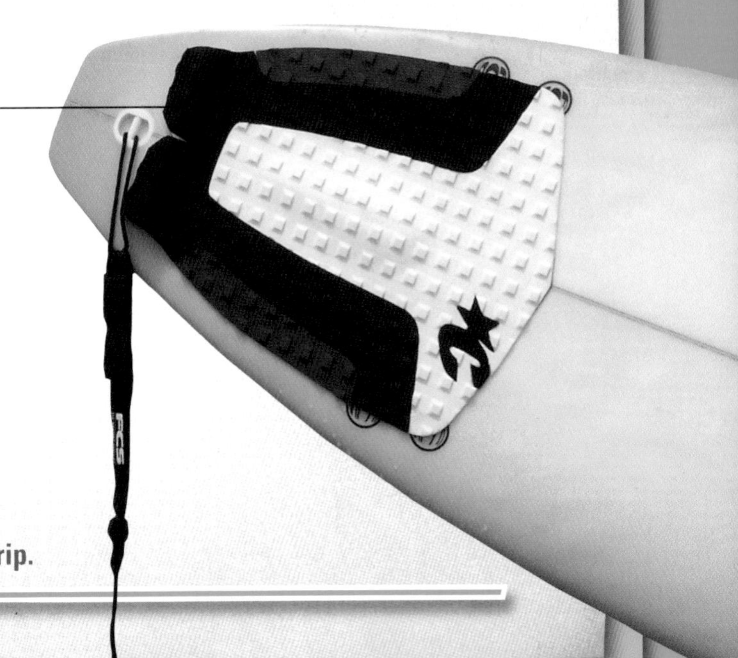


A tailpad gives the surfer extra grip.

# Clothing

A surfing session can last for a number of hours, so surfers need protection from sunburn and, in certain places, the cold water. Surfers wear different clothing in different conditions.

## Wetsuits and rash vests

Wetsuits are made from rubber and vary in length and thickness. There are two types of wetsuits: steamers and springsuits. Steamers have long arms and legs. They are used in cold conditions. Springsuits have short arms and legs. They are used in warm conditions.

Surfers need to protect themselves from sunburn and chest rash, especially in summer. They do this by wearing a rash vest. A rash vest is made from **lycra** that blocks out the sun, and is very comfortable to wear. Surfers also wear boardshorts with their rash vests to protect themselves from rashes on their inner thighs.

**Did you know?**

***The first wetsuit was made by two Australian surfers, Doug Warbrick and Brian Singer, who wanted to keep warm in the cold water at Bells Beach, Victoria. Their company, Rip Curl, is now one of the largest in the surf industry.***

**Surfers can choose to wear springsuits or steamers.**

## Flippers

A pair of flippers is an important piece of equipment for bodyboard riders. A bodyboard is short and does not float as well as a surfboard. Using the arms to paddle is often not enough to catch fast-moving waves, so bodyboarders need flippers to give them extra power. Bodyboarders attach their flippers to their ankles with straps called flipper-savers.

## Booties

In very cold water or when surfing near a reef, surfers can wear rubber boots for added warmth and protection. These boots are commonly known as booties.

## Helmets

Many surfers wear helmets to prevent head injury during wipe-outs. Helmets also protect surfers if they are hit by runaway boards.

**Rule**

*In surfing competitions, all surfers need to wear brightly coloured rash vests so that they can be identified by the judges and spectators.*

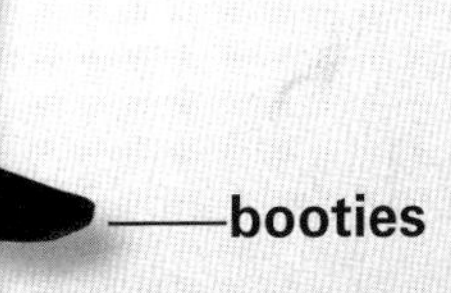


**Booties keep the surfer's feet warm and protect against injury from a reef.**

# Waves

Waves are formed by strong winds and storms far out at sea. The waves are also known as swell. Swell moves towards land and, as the water gets shallow at sandbars and rocky points, the waves 'jack up' and break. Waves usually come in **sets** of four or five. The spot where waves consistently break is called the **line-up** or the break.

## Parts of a wave

All good waves have an obvious peak, where the wave first breaks. The wave breaks as the **lip** of the wave curls over onto the face, creating **wash**. The wash breaks slowly to the right and left of the peak along the length of the wave. The section of wave closest to the breaking wash is the steepest, and is called the **critical section**. Surfers aim to stay in the critical section for as long as they can, so that they can use the wave's power and speed to perform manoeuvres and tricks. The surface of an unbroken wave is called the face or wall. A wave finishes by closing out, where all parts of the wave break and turn into wash. This makes the wave unrideable.

The features of a surf break

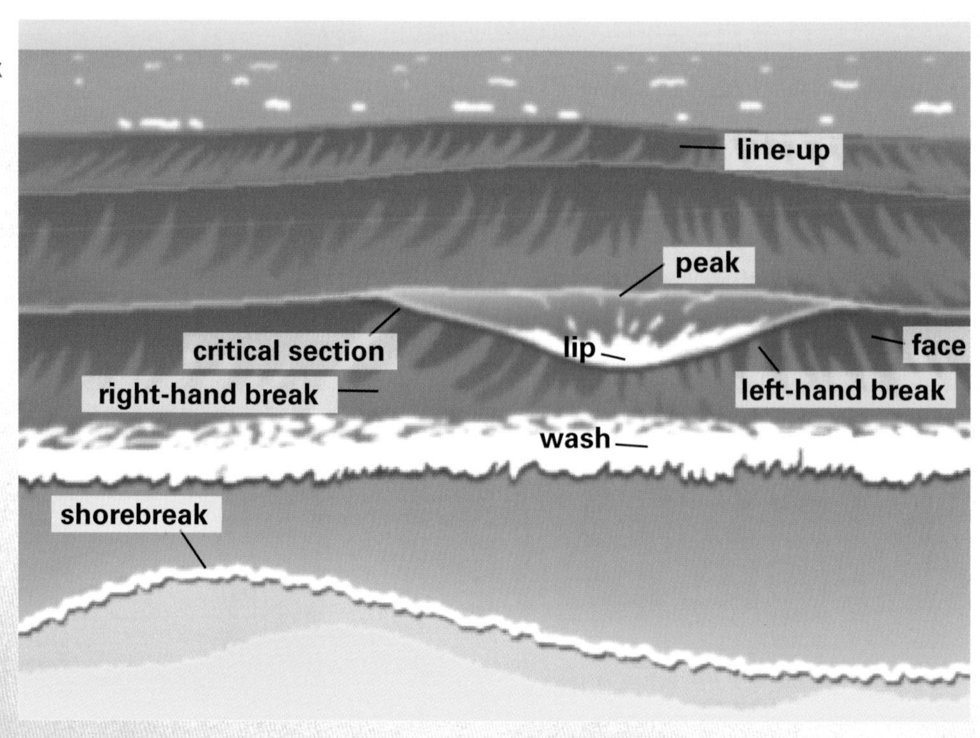

## Types of surf breaks

The shape of the ocean floor and the shoreline determine the type of waves that make up each surf break. There are three main types of surf breaks: beach break, point break and reef break.



### Beach break

Beach break waves break over a bottom of compacted sand, known as a sandbar. Beach break waves are less consistent than waves that break over reefs, and can break in all directions, sizes and shapes. Beach break waves are the most common type of surf break and are the best place for surfers to develop their skills.

**This is a perfect beach break wave.**

### Point break

Point break waves break in the shallow water that surrounds an outcrop of land, known as a point or headland. These waves break over a sandy or rocky bottom and can provide surfers with very long rides.

**Point break waves wrap around the point at Snapper Rocks in Queensland.**

### Reef break

At a reef break, the waves break over a coral reef or rock shelf. Reef waves are usually very powerful and break in shallow water. They are often steep and can become hollow. This allows surfers to become covered up by the lip of the wave, which is called getting tubed. Reef breaks are only for experienced surfers because the waves are powerful and the bottom is dangerous.

# Surfing skills

Surfing involves many different skills, from basic techniques to more advanced manoeuvres. With practice, surfers try to master these skills.

## Paddling

Paddling is the most basic surfing skill but it is also the most important. A strong paddler can catch waves with ease and paddle out to the line-up as quickly as possible.

When paddling, the surfer lies on the board and tries to stay centred. When comfortable, the surfer arches the back and uses a stroke similar to freestyle swimming to move forward. The key to good, strong paddling is to use even, alternating strokes.

**The correct paddling technique**

## Duck-diving

Duck-diving is a skill used to make paddling out to the line-up easier. The aim of the duck-dive is to avoid being thrown around by a broken wave by ducking underneath it. To complete a duck-dive, the surfer follows these steps.

**The duck-dive**

1 As the white water approaches, the surfer grabs both rails of the board and arches the back.

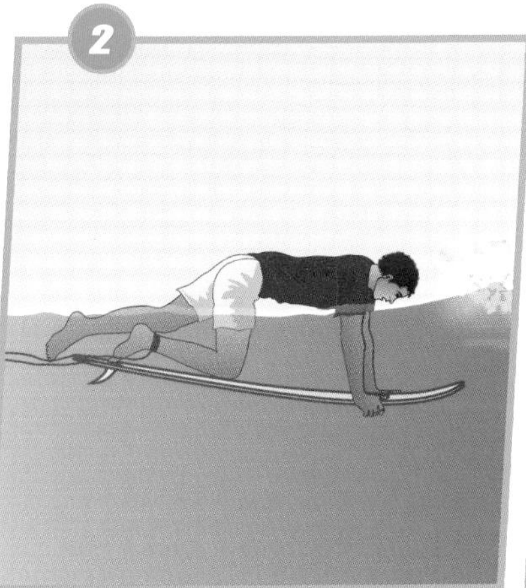


2 Next, the surfer pushes the nose of the board underneath the water's surface and brings one knee up to push the rest of the board under.

3 The surfer ducks under the water and pushes the board down while diving downwards.

4 Once underwater, the surfer lies flat on the board and allows the wave to pass overhead.

5 When the wave has passed, the surfer uses both arms to guide the board back to the surface and continues paddling.

## Taking off

Taking off is the technique of paddling onto a wave and standing up. It is the next important skill for the surfer to master. The take-off is done in a continuous, quick motion. To take off successfully, the surfer follows these steps.

**Taking off**

1 When a wave approaches, the surfer turns and paddles at an angle towards the beach. The nose of the board points in the direction the surfer will ride.

2 When the wave picks the board up, the surfer brings both hands back level with the shoulders and rests them on either rail.

3 Next, the surfer arches the back and does a push-up with both arms until they are straight.

4 The surfer quickly brings the front foot under the chest and places it in the middle of the deck with the knee bent.

5 Putting the most weight on the front foot, the surfer slides the back foot onto the tail of the board and stands up. The surfer keeps both knees slightly bent and uses the arms for balance.

**Rule**

*In a competition, if a surfer takes off on a wave that an opponent is already riding, the surfer will be penalised for interference and will lose points.*

## The stance

There are two different stances for riding a surfboard. Surfers choose whichever one feels most comfortable. The stances are:

- **natural foot** – riding with the left foot forward
- **goofy foot** – riding with the right foot forward.

Both natural and goofy foot surfers can ride either **forehand** or **backhand**. When riding forehand, the surfer faces the wave. When riding backhand, the surfer faces away from the wave.

This surfer is riding forehand in the natural foot stance.

## Trimming

**Trimming** is riding along the face of the wave. It is one of the most important skills for a surfer to master. Once up and riding, the surfer angles the board across the wave by shifting the bodyweight over the rail that is closest to the wave face. The surfer can then centre the bodyweight and ride along the face of the wave.

## Bottom turn

The surfer needs to perform a bottom turn when the speed and power of the wave make it difficult to go from standing up to trimming across the wave face in one easy movement. A good bottom turn sets up the rest of the surfer's ride.

To perform a bottom turn, the surfer transfers the bodyweight to the rail that is closest to the wave face while racing down the face of the wave. The surfer moves onto the toes if riding forehand and onto the heels if riding backhand. On reaching the bottom of the wave, the surfer keeps both knees bent and leans towards the wave face, putting the most weight on the front of the back foot. The board begins to turn towards the wave face. By shifting the weight directly over both feet, the surfer can start trimming across the wave face.

**The bottom turn brings the surfer onto the wave face.**

**Did you know?**

***Jet skis can be used to tow surfers into waves that are up to 15 metres high. When catching waves this big, surfers need to make smooth bottom turns so that they do not wipe-out or lose speed.***

## Top turn

A top turn, or re-entry, is a turn completed at the top of the wave. The aim of the turn is to stop the surfer from flying off the back of the wave by changing direction back down the face of the wave. To perform a top turn, the surfer follows these steps.

**The top turn**

1 Using the speed generated by a good bottom turn, the surfer aims the nose of the board up the wave's face towards the unbroken lip.

2 On reaching the top of the wave, the surfer turns the head and shoulders and points the body back toward the bottom of the wave.

3 The surfer plants the bodyweight on the back foot and uses the front foot to bring the nose of the board around so that it points back down the wave.

4 The surfer then places the bodyweight evenly over both feet and continues riding along the wave face.

## Cutback

Surfers need to perform a cutback when they get too far ahead of the wash. The surfer's main aim when riding a wave is to stay in the critical section. A cutback is a 180-degree turn that brings the surfer back to the critical section without losing speed. To perform a cutback, the surfer follows these steps.

**The cutback**

1 Using the speed from a fast take-off, the surfer performs a powerful bottom turn and heads back up the wave face.

2 At the top of the wave, the surfer puts the bodyweight on both heels, and twists the upper body to look back towards the wash.

3 The surfer leans on the back foot and brings the board and the legs back under the upper body, pointing back towards the wash.

4 The surfer then trims back towards the wash, turns again and continues riding in the critical section.

## Tube riding

The **tube**, or barrel, is a tunnel of water produced by a powerful wave breaking in shallow water. Tube riding is quite a difficult skill to master, and is an exciting surfing experience. When tube riding, surfers need to:

- take off close to the peak
- watch the lip
- control their speed using the back foot. This allows the lip of the wave to pitch over the top of the surfer.

Tube riding takes a lot of practice to master.

**Did you know?**

*In the 2005 World Championship Tour final in Tahiti, six-time world champion American Kelly Slater received two perfect 10 scores for tube riding.*

## Floater

When performing a floater, surfers use their speed to skim or float across the breaking lip of the wave. A floater is an impressive-looking manoeuvre, performed at high speed. Surfers use floaters to get around a section of wave that is breaking in front of them. When performing a floater, surfers need to:

- ride high on the wave face
- aim the nose of the board across the top of a breaking section
- bend both knees and use light footwork.

A surfer floats across the breaking lip of a wave.

# Bodyboarding skills

Bodyboarding has its own special set of skills. With practice, bodyboarders try to master these skills.

## Taking off

Learning to take off and catch waves successfully is the first and most important skill for a bodyboarder to master. When taking off, the bodyboarder chooses a wave to catch, then begins kicking both legs and paddling towards shore. If going right, the bodyboarder paddles with the left arm and puts the right hand on the nose of the board. If going left, the bodyboarder does the opposite. When the wave picks the board up, the bodyboarder uses the paddling arm to grab about halfway up the rail that is furthest from the wave face. Arching the back, the bodyboarder leans in the direction of the turn. Now the bodyboarder can trim across the open wave face, using the wave's speed and power.

**Did you know?**

***American Tom Morey created the first bodyboard in 1971. After breaking his surfboard, he used a carving knife and an iron to turn a scrap piece of foam into a rectangular surf mat.***

**A bodyboarder needs to learn to take off on a wave before mastering other bodyboarding skills.**

# Cutback

Bodyboard cutbacks are used for the same reason as surfing cutbacks. The bodyboarder performs a cutback to return to the steepest and most critical part of the wave. To perform a cutback, the bodyboarder follows these steps.

**The bodyboard cutback**

1 The bodyboarder rides high on the wave, then shifts the bodyweight to the rail furthest from the wave face and begins to turn down the wave.

2 While pushing through the turn with the hips, the bodyboarder uses the hands to guide the nose of the board back towards the wash.

3 At the base of the wave, the bodyboarder centres the bodyweight on the board to get ready to continue the ride.

4 The bodyboarder then performs a bottom turn and continues the ride.

## Spin

The spin or 360 is a basic, but useful manoeuvre. Bodyboarders perform spins to return to the most critical part of the wave, and also because they are a lot of fun. To complete a spin, the bodyboarder follows these steps.

**The spin**

1 The bodyboarder starts the turn by placing the bodyweight over the rail that is closest to the wave face.

2 The bodyboarder begins to slide forward on the board and uses the momentum from the turn to spin smoothly on the wave face.

3 When spinning, the bodyboarder arches the back, bends both knees and brings the flippers out of the water.

4 The bodyboarder rotates until facing the shore, then shifts the bodyweight back and continues riding in the critical section of the wave.

# Aerials

Aerials are spectacular manoeuvres in which the bodyboarder launches off the lip into midair before landing back on the wave face. To perform an aerial, the bodyboarder follows these steps.

**A bodyboard aerial**

**1** Using maximum speed, the bodyboarder performs a powerful bottom turn and aims the board back up the wave towards the lip. On reaching the top of the wave, the bodyboarder aims to hit the lip just as the wave begins to break.

**2** The bodyboarder launches into the air, twisting the body and using the arms to aim the board back towards the beach.

**3** The bodyboarder picks a landing spot on the wave face and brings the board back to a horizontal position, before landing back on the wave.

**4** When landing back on the wave, the bodyboarder makes sure both elbows are bent. This cushions the stomach from the impact of landing.

# Rules and safety

Following these rules and safety tips makes surfing more enjoyable as it helps surfers avoid unnecessary accidents.

## The golden rule

The most important rule for surfers is known as the golden rule. The golden rule says that there can be only one surfer to a wave. The surfer who is closest to the peak has the right of way and other surfers cannot **drop in** on that surfer. This helps avoid collisions.

## Safe paddling

When paddling out, surfers need to avoid paddling through the critical section so that they do not get run over by other surfers. Surfers paddle out wide and, when level with the line-up, paddle across to the peak.

**Other surfers need to wait if there is already one surfer on a wave.**

## Controlling the board

To avoid hitting swimmers and other surfers with the board, surfers need to use a leg-rope or leash. When in the waves, whether paddling out or duck-diving, surfers also need to try to hang onto the board.

## More surfing safety tips

Only competent swimmers should learn to surf. Completing a swimming certificate is a good idea. Surfers should always surf with a friend. They also need to be aware of dangers in the water, such as sharks and jellyfish. They need to avoid surfing at shark feeding times, such as dusk and dawn.

Surfers need to study the surf carefully for hidden dangers before going in. They need to look out for rips, rocks and reefs. A rip is a channel of water moving out to sea. Getting caught in a rip can be very dangerous. Rips can usually be spotted by the lines of foam heading out to sea. Surfers also need to learn how to wipe-out the right way by falling into the wave and never falling headfirst.

Rips are very dangerous and need to be avoided at all costs.

**Rule**

*Surfers need to follow the instructions of beach lifeguards. A lifeguard may ask surfers to move up or down the beach because they are surfing in a dangerous area, and may be close to rocks or a rip.*

# Surfing fitness

Surfboard riding and bodyboarding are excellent for general fitness. Surfers need to be fit, strong and flexible, and have good heart and lung power. To get the most out of their sessions, surfers need to warm up and cool down.

## Warming up and cooling down

Before a surfing session, it is very important that surfers' joints and muscles are loose and warm. A good warm-up on the beach gets surfers' muscles warm and stretched before they enter the water. A cool-down stretches the muscles out after surfing. Surfers are also less likely to be injured after stretching.

### Shoulder stretch

With one hand, the surfer reaches behind their neck and as far down their back as possible. With the other hand, the surfer slowly puts pressure on the elbow of the arm that is being stretched. The surfer holds the shoulder stretch for 30 seconds, then swaps arms.

### Quad stretch

The surfer stands with one leg straight and the other bent and raised behind. With one hand, the surfer reaches behind and slowly pulls the foot of the bent leg up towards the buttocks. This stretches the quadriceps muscle, or quad, which is the large muscle on the front of the thigh. The surfer holds the stretch for 30 seconds, then swaps legs.

Surfers need to stretch their arms and backs before a surfing session.

### Leg roll

The surfer lies on their back with both arms spread wide, one leg straight and one leg bent. Slowly, the surfer rolls the bent leg across and over the straight leg, keeping the shoulders flat on the ground. The surfer touches the ground with the bent knee and holds this position for 30 seconds, before repeating the roll to the other side.

### Seated hamstring stretch

Sitting with one leg straight and the other leg bent to the side, the surfer bends forward at the waist and slowly slides both hands down the straight leg as far as possible. This stretches the hamstring of the straight leg, which runs down the back of the thigh and behind the knee. The surfer holds the stretch for 30 seconds, then swaps legs.

### Calf stretch

The surfer stands close to a wall, fence or other object. Resting both hands on the object, the surfer places one leg further back than the other. Keeping the heel of the back foot on the ground and bending the front knee, the surfer slowly bends both arms and leans in toward the object. The surfer feels the stretch in the calf muscle of the straight leg. The surfer holds the stretch for 30 seconds, then swaps legs.

**The surfer holds each stretch, such as the calf stretch, for 30 seconds.**

### Trunk stretch

The surfer lies face-down with both hands under the shoulders and both legs straight. The surfer slowly straightens the arms and arches the back, keeping both thighs flat on the ground so that the trunk is fully stretched. The surfer holds the stretch for 30 seconds, then lowers the trunk back to the ground.

# Competition

Every year, surfing competitions are held at beaches all over the world. During summer, many local surf clubs organise surfing competitions for female and male surfers of all ages. A number of countries also run state and national surfing championships, including Australia and the United States of America. In some surfing competitions, surfers compete as part of a team that represents either their surf club or their state or country, but in most competitions surfers compete for themselves.

## World Championship Tour

The pinnacle of all surfing competitions is the World Championship Tour (WCT), which is run by the Association of Surfing Professionals (ASP). The WCT runs for 10 months of the year. It is for the world's best male and female surfers. During the tour, surfers compete in 12 tournaments that are held at beaches all over the world, including Australia, Hawaii, Japan and the United States.

**The first, second and third placegetters in professional surfing championships are given awards.**

## Surfing competition rules

Most surfing competitions are 'knock-out' tournaments. Surfers compete in heats against one or three other surfers. The heats last for up to 30 minutes. At the end of the heat, the surfer with the highest point score progresses to the next round of the competition. In competitions, surfers are identified by the colours of their rash vests.

During the heat, surfers try to catch as many good waves as they can, however, only the two or three highest scoring waves count towards their total score. A panel of five judges give each surfer a score out of 10 for each wave they catch. Points are awarded to each surfer for:

- the size and quality of the waves they choose to ride
- the number of tricks the surfer performs
- how well the surfer performs those tricks
- the length of the ride
- the amount of 'tube time' the surfer gets.

**Rule**

*In World Championship Tour contests, the first surfer to paddle out to the line-up has priority. This means that they have the first pick of the waves and their opponent must wait.*

**Competing surfers are awarded points if they perform tricks successfully.**

# Looking after the environment

Surfers can help look after the environment and continue to enjoy clear water, clean beaches and coastal wildlife. They can make sure rubbish is not left on the beach. Rubbish pollutes the water and can harm marine life. Plastic bags can be swallowed and block the intestines of sea birds, mammals and fish.

Surfers can also help protect the environment by caring for sand dunes. Sand dunes are held together by plants. If the plants are removed or trampled on, the sand dunes blow away. Surfers can avoid damaging plants by walking or driving on marked tracks when going to or from the beach. Surfers can also care for water when they are at home. Most coastal pollution starts on the land. Rubbish, dog faeces and oil on the road or streets are washed into drains and eventually out to sea. Surfers can care for their home environments as well as for the beach by not dropping litter and never washing pollutants down the drain.

**All surfers can enjoy clean beaches if they help to look after the environment.**

**Did you know?**

***Each year, around 7 billion tonnes of rubbish is dumped into oceans worldwide. This has a devastating effect on ocean environments.***

# Glossary



**backhand** surfing with your back to the wave

**critical section** the section of wave closest to the breaking wash; the steepest and fastest part of the wave

**deck** the top of a surfboard or bodyboard

**drop in** to take off on a wave that someone else is already riding; this is against the rules of surfing

**face** the unbroken, smooth part of the wave; also known as the wall

**fibreglass** a hard, see-through coating, which is used to protect the foam core of a surfboard

**forehand** surfing with your face and chest facing the wave

**goofy foot** standing on the surfboard with the right foot forward

**line-up** the area where most of the waves break

**lip** the leading edge of a breaking wave

**lycra** an elastic, skin-tight fabric used in surfing rash vests

**natural foot** standing on the surfboard with the left foot forward

**peak** the part of the wave that breaks first

**rails** the sides of a surfboard or bodyboard deck

**sets** groups of waves that break quickly, one after the other

**trimming** riding along the face of a wave

**tube** a tunnel of water produced by a powerful wave breaking in shallow water; also known as a barrel

**wash** the messy white water that a wave turns into after it has broken

**wipe-out** to fall or get knocked off the surfboard

# Index